TRADES To the RESCUE!

When the Lights Go Out, the Fixers Gear Up.

Written by Archie D. Nettles, Jr.

Illustrated by TullipStudio

This book is dedicated to my father, Archie D. Nettles, Sr., my mother, Alice Dent Nettles, my sisters, nieces, nephews and extended family, friends, and all the families and children in small-town America, where trades thrive and dreams come alive.

ZIIING!

Welcome to TradesTopolis, a place where skilled hands build brighter futures. Meet Torque and Tori, two best friends who love to fix, create, and explore the trades that power their world.

ZIIING!

Torque, with his trusty wrench, and Tori,
with her magnetic drill, always solve problems and
build dreams with teamwork and skill.

In the heart of TradesTopolis lies Trades Town, a lively place where everyone plays a role: electricians, plumbers, builders, and more.

ZIIING!

ZIIING!

Sunrise in Trades Town means tools clicking, sparks flying, and ideas coming to life. Everyone starts the day with joy and purpose.

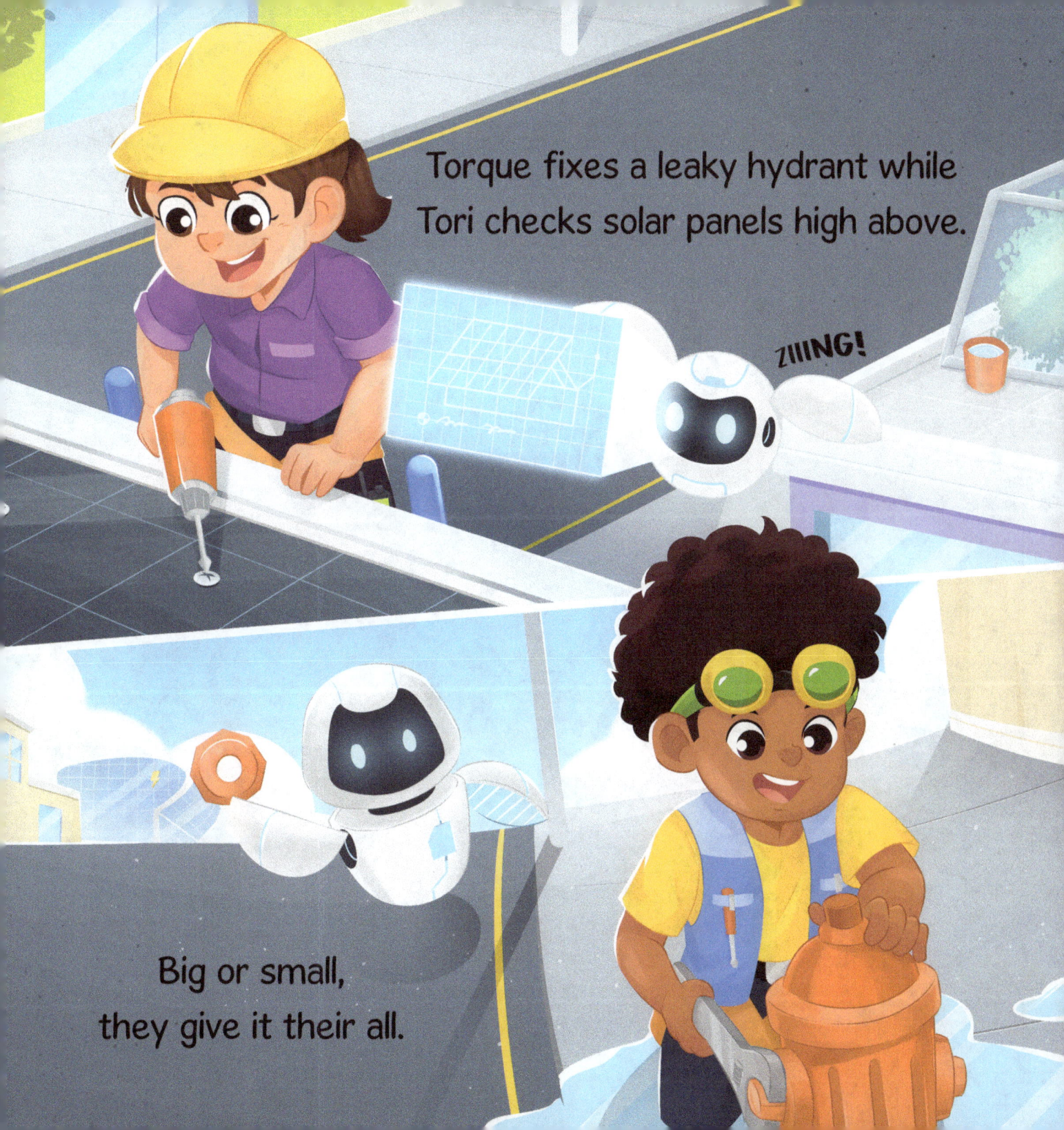

Trades Town is full of work and play. Tonight, they celebrate Trades Day.

Tonight is the festival,
big and bright. Lanterns glow
and kites take flight.

Suddenly, ZAP! A FLASH! A BOOM!
Darkness fills the town with gloom.

Tori shouts, "To the power station,
let's go fast! I will trace the wires
and run the path."

Torque grabs the toolkit.
"And I'll check the panels.
We've got to bring the lights back!"

Electricity flows in a steady stream,
from power plants to homes
that flicker and gleam.

Torque twists. Tori holds tight.
SPARK, SPARK, ZAP!
Then... LIGHT!

The festival glows. The people cheer.
Torque and Tori save the year.
They fixed the lights with skill and grace,
Teamwork shining all over the place.

Mayor Gearsby shakes their hands.
"Great job, you two. You saved our plans!"

Builders, welders, electricians, and engineers work hard to fix problems and make things new.

Torque and Tori unroll a blueprint wide.
"This design will help the town with pride.
Once we build it, no more delays.
We'll brighten up all future days!"

Trades are the tools the world needs to grow. Let's see which trade you'll want to know.

Electricians light the way,
wiring homes where children play.

Plumbers make sure water flows through every faucet, pipe, and hose.

Carpenters hammer, saw, and frame, building spaces that earn their name.

Welders wear masks and sparks fly high. They shape the steel that scrapes the sky.

Heating, Ventilation, and Air Conditioner (HVAC) techs keep comfort in place, warm in winter, cool every space.

Crane operators lift with grace,
moving beams into their place.

ZIIING!

ZIIING!

Mechanics fix with tools and might,
so cars and trucks run day and night.

TradesTopolis needs heroes like you,
With steady hands and a dream or two.

ZIIING!

So pick up your tools, your helmet, your gloves.
Join the trades and do what you love.
The world needs your spark to shine bright.
In TradesTopolis, every job feels just right.

ZIIING!

Safety Tips and Learning
Torque & Tori's Top Safety Tips
Let's Stay Safe While We Build!

Hi, Fix-It Friend!
Torque and Tori love to explore, build, and learn,
but they always put safety first,
especially when it comes to electricity. You should too!

Top 5 Safety Rules

Don't Touch Wires!

1

See a wire that's broken or hanging?
Tell a grown-up right away!

Dry Hands, Safe Hands!

2

Never use tools or touch plugs with
wet hands. Water and electricity
do not mix!

Always Ask First!

3

Before flipping a switch or plugging
something in, ask an adult to help.

Top 5 Safety Rules

Gear Up!

4

Put on your safety goggles, gloves, and thinking cap before you build!

Stop. Look. Then Fix!

5

Think before you touch. Be smart and safe like Torque and Tori!

Words We Learned

- **Circuit** – A path that electricity travels through

- **Current** – The flow of electricity (like a tiny river!)

- **Plug** – What connects something to power

- **Shock** – A little zap from touching something unsafe

- **Tool** – Something that helps you fix or build

Fix-It Glossary: Words & Wonders

- **Circuit** – A loop that powers things like lights and TVs
- **Toolbox** – A home for screwdrivers, wrenches, and more
- **Voltage** – The push that moves electricity through wires
- **Tinker** – To explore how something works by building or fixing
- **Power Outage** – When the lights suddenly go out

Fix-It Glossary: Words & Wonders

- **Electrician** – A pro who keeps the lights on and homes safe
- **Generator** – A backup machine that makes power when there is none
- **Blueprint** – A special drawing that shows how to build something
- **Trade Skills** – Hands-on jobs like fixing, wiring, building, and plumbing
- **Fuse** – A tiny part that stops circuits from getting too hot
- **Tek & Trek** – Tiny, talking tool buddies
- **TradesTopolis** – A magical fix-it city powered by teamwork and tools

Tool	What It Does
Screwdriver	Turns screws in or out
Wrench	Loosens or tightens nuts and bolts
Pliers	Holds or pinches small things
Flashlight	Helps you see in the dark
Multimeter	Checks how electricity is working

Activity Page: Build Your Dream Tool belt!

Draw and label the tools you would put in your tool belt.
Pick a trade that excites you, then
create a picture and name for your first invention.

Tool belt Template: _____   Trade: _____

My Tool Names:

1. _____   2. _____   3. _____

Bonus Challenge:

What Will You Build?
Every great inventor starts with one simple question:

"How can I help my community?"
Now it's your turn!

Think of something your town, school, or neighborhood needs, then imagine a tool, machine, or invention you could build to fix it. Be bold. Be creative. Be you.

Sketch your idea in the space below and give it a name!

- -

Name of My Creation: -

What It Does: -

- -

- -

- -

Great builders make big changes, one idea at a time.

What will YOU build next?

- -

About the Author

Archie D. Nettles, Jr. is a proud Army veteran, public speaker, community leader, and children's book author with a heart for big dreams and hardworking hands. Raised in Southeast Texas, he grew up watching his father, uncles, and neighbors work with pride in trades like plumbing, wiring, welding, and building things by hand.

This book is a tribute to the memory of the late Archie D. Nettles Sr. (his father), Benny Nettles Sr. (his uncle), and his grandfather Hillman Guillory. These men laid the foundation for his journey.

His grandfather Ardie Nettles, Uncle Troy Dent, and other uncles also inspired this book and continue to be living examples of grit, wisdom, and quiet strength.

Archie also dedicates this book to the everyday heroes, whether family or not, who still ask, "How does that process work?"

To the curious, the builders, and the doers. Thank you for lighting the path. The future is not inherited. It is built.

His stories celebrate curiosity, community, and the power of learning to build a brighter world one spark at a time.